Housekeeper Wanted

A Farce

Philip King and
Falkland L. Cary

A Samuel French Acting Edition

FOUNDED 1830

SAMUELFRENCH-LONDON.CO.UK
SAMUELFRENCH.COM

Copyright © 1972 by Philip King and Falkland L. Cary
All Rights Reserved

HOUSEKEEPER WANTED is fully protected under the copyright laws of the British Commonwealth, including Canada, the United States of America, and all other countries of the Copyright Union. All rights, including professional and amateur stage productions, recitation, lecturing, public reading, motion picture, radio broadcasting, television and the rights of translation into foreign languages are strictly reserved.

ISBN 978-0-573-12111-1

www.samuelfrench-london.co.uk

www.samuelfrench.com

For Amateur Production Enquiries

United Kingdom and World excluding North America

plays@SamuelFrench-London.co.uk

020 7255 4302/01

Each title is subject to availability from Samuel French, depending upon country of performance.

CAUTION: Professional and amateur producers are hereby warned that HOUSEKEEPER WANTED is subject to a licensing fee. Publication of this play does not imply availability for performance. Both amateurs and professionals considering a production are strongly advised to apply to the appropriate agent before starting rehearsals, advertising, or booking a theatre. A licensing fee must be paid whether the title is presented for charity or gain and whether or not admission is charged.

The professional rights in this play are controlled by Samuel French Ltd, 52 Fitzroy Street, London, W1T 5JR.

No one shall make any changes in this title for the purpose of production. No part of this book may be reproduced, stored in a retrieval system, or transmitted in any form, by any means, now known or yet to be invented, including mechanical, electronic, photocopying, recording, videotaping, or otherwise, without the prior written permission of the publisher. No one shall upload this title, or part of this title, to any social media websites.

The right of Philip King and Falkland L. Cary to be identified as author of this work has been asserted by them in accordance with Section 77 of the Copyright, Designs and Patents Act 1988

CHARACTERS

Victor
  the victim, who is looking for a housekeeper
Visitor One
Visitor Two
Visitor Three
Visitor Four

The action passes in the lounge of a small suburban house on a day in summer

Time – the present

HOUSEKEEPER WANTED

The lounge of a small suburban house. A day in summer

When the CURTAIN *rises, Victor is on stage—but the only part of him to be seen at the moment is his hindquarters, as he is doing something with a brush and pan underneath the table. First he throws out the brush, and then emerges closely himself with the pan*

Victor is a pleasant-looking young man, but he has a slightly frenzied air which is added to by the fact that he has a duster tied round his head—as he has seen his wife similarly equipped when dusting, etc. As he emerges completely he rises to his feet, holding the pan at such an angle that the contents slide on to the carpet

Victor Blast! (*He bends and hastily and inadequately brushes the debris into the pan again. This done, he puts the pan on a chair with the brush in it and looks round in a highly housewifely fashion. His eyes light on an ashtray crammed full of cigarette ends and matches. He takes this up, looks at it and then makes for the waste-paper basket, but as it is crammed to the full, he shakes his head and looks round for something in which to put the contents of the ashtray. He finally settles for the pan and shoots the contents of the ashtray into it. The problem now is where to dispose of the contents of the pan. He looks round wildly and finally, with a sigh of relief, tips the lot behind the electric fire and automatically, throws the ashtray after it. Looking round the room, his eyes light on a truly hideous ornament on a table. His body gives a convulsive twitch, as if in pain. A look of deadly hatred comes into his eyes. Slowly his body shrinks into a menacing crouching attitude, then he slowly crosses towards the ornament as if "stalking" it. When near the table, his arm darts out and he grasps the ornament and holds it out at arm's length. He regards it with utter loathing. Then suddenly he raises his arm as if to dash the ornament to the ground, but, instead of doing this—his courage having failed him—he spins round in his own tracks, still clutching the ornament firmly. He runs a hand across his brow. Weakly muttering*) Coward! Cowardly Victor. (*He holds the ornament at arm's length again glaring at it. Muttering*) Why don't you, man? Why don't you? Why don't you show her? Victory is in your grasp. How glorious to be victorious! (*A slight pause*) I'll do it! By heaven! I'll do it! (*He places the ornament carefully on the floor, steps back about a yard, then after a slight pause, jumps into the air, but as he goes up, gives a yelp of horror. He comes down, well away from the ornament, gasps with relief, and quickly picks up the ornament in his two shaking hands. He restores the ornament very shakily to the table, then moves away, turns, facing the ornament, shakes his fist at it. Then, pointing a menacing finger towards it*) You wait! Just you wait!

The telephone rings. Victor moves quickly to answer it

(*Into the phone*) Hello-o? (*Pleased*) Oh, the Confidence Unlimited Employment Bureau! Good! What news? . . . (*Delighted*) You are? (*More delighted*) You have? . . . You've sent me a housekeeper in whom you have every confidence. Marvellous! (*Looking round the room*) There's only one snag—she hasn't arrived! . . . She will? Oh, I see. . . . You've every confidence she will. Good—good. . . . What was that? You've every confidence she will suit, but in case she doesn't you're sending me some others in whom you've even *more* confidence. Well, er—confidentially, I . . . Oh, you've rung off! (*To the receiver*) Good-bye! (*He automatically begins singing quietly to himself as he takes the soda syphon from the drinks tray and wipes it with his elbow*)
"Confidentially, I like your smile,
  Confidentially . . ."

Visitor One appears in the doorway. She is any age, a rubicund lady with a large shopping basket from which the neck of a bottle shows. She is colourfully dressed but her manner is anything but colourful

Visitor One (*dolefully*) 'Scuse me!
Victor (*turning in surprise and letting fly a squirt of soda water on the floor*) 'Scuse me, first.
Visitor One You're not '*im*, are you?
Victor (*puzzled*) 'Im? (*Brightly*) Oh, yes! I think I *am*, actually. (*Somewhat alarmed*) You're not '*er* . . . er, *Her*, are you?
Visitor One 'Er?

Housekeeper Wanted 3

Victor (*muttering*) Have it your own way! (*Explaining*) Her—er —HER, from the Confidence Unlimited Employment Bureau.
Visitor One (*nodding*) Ah!
Victor (*to himself*) Pah!
Visitor One (*dolefully*) On the door . . . (*She stops*)
Victor (*puzzled*) I beg your pardon?
Visitor One On the door—I noticed your notice. It said, "Please come in."
Victor Yes—er—it would, really, as that's what I wrote on it.
Visitor One "Please come in," it said.
Victor (*somewhat exasperated*) That's what I said it said.
Visitor One So—shall I come in?

Victor makes a small whinneying noise

If not, you've only got to say.
Victor For God's sake—(*quickly*) I mean, please—*please* come in.
Visitor One (*more dolefully than ever*) Well, you can't say more than that, can you?

Victor almost whimpers. Visitor One steps into the room

I'm in.

Victor unconsciously squirts more soda on the carpet then puts the syphon on the drinks table and hastily wipes the carpet with his handkerchief. Visitor One moves to his side, watching

(*Sadly*) You didn't ought to do that!
Victor You mean you want to do it for me?
Visitor One Nothin' was further from my thoughts. I mean, you didn't ought to wipe carpets with 'ankies, that's not what they're for.
Victor I say, you're not the fussy type, are you?
Visitor One No, I'm not, but I can't stand the filthy type. Are you the filthy type?
Victor (*indignantly*) No, I am not. I'll have you know, I have a bath every morning.
Visitor One (*suspiciously*) Why? What's wrong with you?
Victor *Madam*—I . . . !
Visitor One I mean, 'ave your best friends been 'inting?
Victor I—I . . . (*He wipes the floor furiously*)

Visitor One (*removing the scarf from his head*) 'Ere, use this. It's been on your 'ead, but still ... (*Moving to a small chair*) Mind if I take the weight off me feet?

Victor No, but be careful how you put it on that chair. It's rather fragile.

Visitor One Yes, it is a bit airy-fairy, itsy-bitsy, isn't it? (*After sitting; ponderously*) Well—*now* ...

Victor (*equally ponderously*) Yes—well—*now* ...?

Visitor One Yes, well—*now*.

Victor Yes, well, now ... (*Laughing*) We're both suffering from stuck needles, aren't we? (*He laughs for a while, then suddenly stops*)

Visitor One (*at last; dolefully*) From *what* stuck?

Victor Needles. (*Desperately*) You know, gramophone needles stuck in the record. (*He laughs feebly*)

Visitor One (*apprehensively*) 'Ere, you're not 'umorous, are you?

Victor 'Umour ...?

Visitor One I can't abide 'umour; so if you're 'umorous ...

Victor (*hastily*) Oh, I'm not—and if I was, I can assure you I never shall be again.

Visitor One (*satisfied*) Ah! (*She settles down*)

Victor Well—er—*now!* (*To himself*) Blast! (*Brightly*) References?

Visitor One Wot?

Victor References. You've brought them with you, of course.

Visitor One (*indignantly*) Of course I've done no such thing! I don't 'old with 'em.

Victor No?

Visitor One Wouldn't be seen dead with them. Wot you want old-fashioned things like them for? You want to move with the times. 'Asn't Confidence Unlimited told you they 'ave every——

Victor —*confidence* in you? Yes, they have.

Visitor One Well, 'ere I am. A shinin' example of their confidence. I mean, you've only got to look me over, 'aven't you?

Victor Well—I will! I will! Give me time. (*Muttering*) And strength! (*His eyes fall on the bottle sticking out of the bag*) What I'm looking at at the moment is ...

Visitor One notices just where he is looking and hastily takes a copy of "War Cry" from her coat pocket and covers the bottle

Housekeeper Wanted

(*After this is done*) Er—have Confidence Unbelievable—Unlimited, told you my requirements?
Visitor One Yes, but we'll put *them* right later. First things, first, I always say.
Victor Er—wages. You've been told what they will be?
Visitor One I've been told what you *think* they will be.
Victor But . . .
Visitor One But I'm no sinner, I'd 'ave you know!
Victor (*gaping at her*) I *beg* your pardon?
Visitor One "The wages of sin is death," and that's what you seem to be offering—all the work there'll be 'ere.
Victor Oh, but . . .
Visitor One (*soothingly*) Now, now, not to upset yourself. I 'aven't told you what you can do with the job yet, 'ave I?
Victor I—I . . .
Visitor One No. No, so 'ang on while you can. An' we'll talk about wages later. We'll see 'ow we get on together, eh?
Victor But . . .
Visitor One (*singing in a low quavering voice*) "The more we are together, the 'appier we shall be."
Victor (*muttering*) And *that's* debatable!
Visitor One Pardon?
Victor Granted. It's—it's a small house.
Visitor One 'Ow small?
Victor (*after demonstrating smallness with his hands*) One lounge, dining-room, two bedrooms, bathroom, separate—er—convenience.
Visitor One 'Ow separate? Not down in the garden? No, thanks, not for me. I catch cold easily.
Victor It's . . .
Visitor One (*continuing*) Down the garden, no! I'm no 'iker!
Victor (*testily*) It's in the house.
Visitor One (*dolefully*) I see! More work! (*Suddenly*) 'Ow do you cook?
Victor Abominably. Oh, I see what you mean. You mean *how* do I cook?
Visitor One (*dolefully*) If me memory serves me right, *that's* wot I *said*. 'Ow?
Victor Gas. With gas.
Visitor One Not that nasty North Sea stuff?

Victor I—I suppose I *could* arrange for it to come from the Mediterranean.
Visitor One (*suddenly*) Washin'! Do *I* do the washin'? 'Cos I don't.
Victor But . . .
Visitor One I've sunk low—Gawd knows, I've sunk—but nobody's never caught me washin'.
Victor (*eyeing her*) And I'm sure nobody ever will.
Visitor One (*hand to throat*) Bit 'ot in 'ere, isn't it?
Victor 'Ot?
Visitor One Me throat—a bit parched like—if you get my meaning?
Victor It's filtering through. (*He begins to sniff and moves nearer to, Visitor One*)
Visitor One 'Aven't got a cold, 'ave you?
Victor Only in my feet. (*He continues to sniff*)
Visitor One Wot you sniffin' at?
Victor (*with overdone nonchalance*) Apropos *ab-so*-lutely nothing at all . . . (*He gives a big sniff near Visitor One*) Er—are you teetotal?
Visitor One A total teetotal! (*Looking heavenwards*) May the ceilin' drop down on me if I'm not!
Victor (*looking heavenwards with a yelp of alarm; muttering*) For God's sake, don't chance that a second time! (*He then waves his hand in front of his nose*)
Visitor One (*seeing this*) You can smell something, can't you?
Victor Well—er—since you mention it. . . .
Visitor One Know what it is?
Victor What?
Visitor One It's me.
Victor You're very frank.
Visitor One O-dee-Cologne!
Victor Eau . . . ?
Visitor One My one weakness. (*She pushes the bottles farther into the bag*)
Victor (*sniffing*) You mean your *other* one, surely?
Visitor One (*suddenly*) 'Ere! You married?
Victor At the moment—yes.
Visitor One Ow'd you mean—at the moment?
Victor I shan't be—not much longer, please God and Her Majesty's Divorce Courts.

Housekeeper Wanted

Visitor One You divorcin' *'er?*
Victor I am.
Visitor One Wot grounds—anky-panky?
Victor Cruelty.
Visitor One (*mystified*) 'Er cruel to *you?*

Victor goes to the small table and takes the hideous ornament and brings it down to Visitor One

Victor (*holding out*) Ever seen anything like this before?
Visitor One (*gaping at the ornament*) I never 'ave—and I don't suppose I ever will again. It's the sort of thing that only 'appens to you once in a lifetime. (*Peering at the ornament*) Wot's it supposed to be?
Victor Only God, and possibly the Shah of Persia could tell you.
Visitor One 'Ow did you come by it? You *never* bought it?
Victor (*heavily*) Yesterday was my birthday . . .
Visitor One (*immediately singing quietly in a doleful quavering voice*) " 'Appy birthday to you
    'Appy birthday to you,
    'Appy birthday, dear . . .
(*breaking off; dolefully*) Wot *is* your name?
Victor (*dazedly*) Victor.
Visitor One (*concluding the aria*)
    'Appy birthday, dear Vic*tor*.
    'Appy birthday to you."
(*Settling back with satisfaction*) There!
Victor (*still dazedly*) Thanks, thanks, and ever thanks! But it *was* yesterday—and it was *far* from happy!
Visitor One Oh shame! Wot 'appened?
Victor (*holding out the ornament*) This!
Visitor One T', t', t'. Ruin any birthday, that would.
Victor (*holding out the ornament again*) *As* it was intended to. (*Dramatically*) *This* was my mother-in-law's birthday present to me*!*
Visitor One Gawd! She must 'ate your guts!
Victor She hates every single part of my anatomy.
Visitor One Yes, but—I mean ter say—sendin' you a thing like that! That's goin' *too* far!
Victor Far too far—especially when my wife insisted it should stand on that table (*pointing*) for ever more!

Visitor One And wot did *you* do?
Victor I insisted that it shouldn't.
Visitor One And wot 'appened then?
Victor All hell broke loose. I lost my temper and told her exactly what I thought of her mother, her grandmother, and every one of her female ancestors back to the time of Ethelred the Unready.
Visitor One Oo-er!
Victor It took quite a time—two hours to be precise, and when I'd finished she announced she was leaving me—going back to mother.
Visitor One An' you *let* 'er?
Victor "Let her?" I encouraged her; thanked her for her humanity!
Visitor One And now you're—all alone.
Victor And now I'm—(*with a little sob*)—all alone.
Visitor One (*again the quavering doleful singing*)
    "All alone, by the telephone,
      Waiting for a ring, a ting-a-ling
      All . . ."
Victor (*breaking in*) Please—I beg you!
Visitor One Wot?
Victor My appreciation of opera is, at this moment, at its lowest ebb. In fact, I . . . (*He sobs once more and unconsciously wipes his eyes with the duster—and immediately sneezes*)
Visitor One Bless you!
Victor Thank you. (*Irritably as he feels in his pockets*) Where the hell's my handkerchief?
Visitor One (*producing a small and extremely grimy handkerchief from her pocket and holding it out*) Use this.
Victor (*taking it absently*) Thanks. (*After looking at it in horror, he turns his back on Visitor One and, holding the corner of the handkerchief by finger and thumb, as far away from his nose as possible, gives a fake sneeze and turns back to Visitor One to return the handkerchief*) Thank you. That was a great help.
Visitor One (*dolefully*) You know, all this 'as properly upset me.
Victor What has?
Visitor One In fact, my 'eart's bleedin' for you.
Victor Oh, but . . .
Visitor One (*firmly*) Bleedin', that's what it is. D'you know, I think I'm going off.

Housekeeper Wanted

Victor (*moving eagerly to the door and opening it*) Good! Now you've got your return bus fare . . . ?
Visitor One (*arms flapping*) Water . . . !
Victor What?
Visitor One Water! I'm goin'! Water! (*She leans back, eyes closed*)
Victor (*panicking*) Oh, my . . . ! (*He closes the door, rushes down, looks at Visitor One for a moment and then begins to rush wildly around*) Water! Water! (*Noticing a cut glass vase with flowers in it*) Ah, water! (*He immediately throws flowers on to table and brings down the vase—which is only half filled with extremely yellow water—and holds it out to Visitor One*) Water! (*Noticing yellowness of water, he gives a little yelp of horror*) Hang on! I'll get some fresh!

Victor rushes out with the vase

After he has gone, Visitor One revives quickly, looks towards the door, then quickly produces a whisky bottle from her bag, unscrews it and puts it to her lips. Her head tilts back further and further in her efforts to drink. At last she removes the bottle from her lips, angrily turns it upside down and shakes it, slaps the bottom of the bottle

Visitor One (*angrily*) Ber-last! (*She fumes for a moment, then looks towards the drinks table, goes to it, bottle still in hand, picks up a whisky bottle with the same label as her own, puts her empty one down, and is about to unscrew the top from the other one when Victor's voice is heard off*)
Victor (*off; brightly*) Here we are!

Visitor One rushes down to the chair, sits, then realizing she is still holding Victor's bottle, slips it quickly into her bag, by the side of the chair

Victor enters carrying the vase, now filled with clean water

Victor (*as he enters*) Here we are! (*He comes down to Visitor One and holds out the vase to her*) Wakey-wakey!

Visitor One gives a loud groan, opens her eyes blearily, and takes the vase from Victor

There's more where that came from. Don't be modest. (*He moves up to the drinks table*)

Visitor One is gazing dolefully into the vase

Visitor One (*dolefully*) Peculiar tastin' stuff, water, isn't it?

Victor (*picking up a sherry bottle*) So I'm told. I prefer sherry myself.

Visitor One Ah, that's just what you need. Sherry never did nobody any 'arm; in fact—do you good—er—so they tell me.

Victor (*holding up the bottle and looking at it*) Damn!

Visitor One Wot?

Victor It's not going to do me any good. Bottle's empty.

Visitor One Ooooh—isn't that vexin'!

Victor Maddening.

Visitor One Yerse! I was maddened just now when I found my bot . . . (*She breaks off, coughing loudly*)

Victor You should take something for that croup.

Visitor One I will—later.

Victor (*putting down the sherry bottle*) Well, no sherry, so—it'll have to be whisky.

Visitor One (*with a yelp*) What!

Victor (*placidly*) Whisky. (*He picks up an empty glass*)

Visitor One (*rising and picking up the glass*) No, no! I can't let you.

Victor (*grinning*) You try and stop me!

Visitor One (*unthinking*) I 'ave! (*Thinking*) I mean—you didn't ought to! Whisky—it'll be the death of you!

Victor What a lovely death! (*He makes to pick up the whisky bottle*)

Visitor One (*stopping him by grabbing his arm*) Don't—don't do it, I beg you, don't. Shall I go on my knees?

Victor I'd rather you didn't.

Visitor One (*quoting*) Then it's "Good-bye for ever. Good-bye, good-bye".

Victor (*lightly*) Cheerio! (*He waves a "paw"*)

Visitor One (*with dignity*) I 'ave my principles, I 'ope.

Victor Oh, I hope so. Do make sure you haven't left them lying around. (*He looks round curiously*)

Visitor One (*with dignity*) I 'ave my principles and they say "*No!*"

Housekeeper Wanted

Victor (*puzzled*) No what?
Visitor One "No, you don't!"
Victor (*puzzled*) But I haven't.
Visitor One "No, you don't," they say. "Live under the same roof as a whisky drinker? Never!" they say. "If you can't pluck a brand from the burning, then leave it to burn itself out!" An' that's just what I'm going to leave you to do. Good morning.
Victor What? Oh—er—arriverderci, Roma.
Visitor One Same to you—and the name's Kathleen. (*As she moves to the door she sings brightly*)
"My drink is water bright,
Water bright,
Water bright,
My drink is . . .

Visitor One exits, still singing

Victor (*also singing, as he "pours" from Visitor One's bottle*) "*My* drink is water bright," etc. etc. (*He is not looking at the glass as he pours. He puts the bottle down puts the glass to his lips, tilting it further and further back, trying to drink*) What the devil . . . ! (*He sees the glass is empty and picks up the bottle to look at it*) But this is damned ridiculous! I only opened it last night! I—(*he turns the bottle upside down*)—I—I only—I swear I only . . . (*He suddenly realizes the truth and with a yelp of rage he darts towards the door*) Come back! Come back, you thieving old faggot!

Visitor Two appears in the doorway. Visitor Two is decidedly "Something"—with a capital S. In the twenties, very sophisticated, wearing the briefest of brief mini-skirts, scarlet boots (up to her thighs), long "ironed" ash blonde hair, eyelashes which God did not give her, and bosoms which, if He did, prove how generous he can be at times. Her voice is low and reeks of "sex". Altogether, breath-taking, and she immediately takes Victor's eye (*Goggling*) Good—God!
Visitor Two (*after looking Victor over and liking what she sees*) Oh! Well—of course . . . ! (*Her eyelashes flutter—and flutter*)
Victor (*almost speechless*) Er—er—er—are you . . . ?

Visitor Two (*still looking him over*) I am. And are *you* . . . ?
Victor (*almost wildly*) Oh, yes! Definitely!
Visitor Two (*huskily*) They told me at the Agency you *would* be.
Victor (*gulping*) How right they were! Excuse me a moment. (*He waves her into the room, then dashes to the phone, quickly dials a number, and then—while waiting, can only gaze and gaze at Visitor Two. Into the phone, with eyes still on her*) Is that the Confidence Unlimited Employment Bureau? . . . It is? Good! My name is—(*eyeing Visitor Two*)—my name is—I can't think *what* my name is at the moment. I have other things on my mind. But I live at—I live at—oh, what's it matter where I live? I just want to say, "Thank you *very* much!" I have every confidence that you've sent me . . .

Visitor Two approaches Victor and gently puts a hand over his which is holding the receiver

Visitor Two (*almost purring*) Not so fast—babe . . .
Victor (*almost in a trance; aware of her hand over his*) M'mmmm-mmmmmm?
Visitor Two We've got to talk—haven't we?
Victor (*goggling*) oh, yes—yes—yes—*talk*—and *after* that . . . ?
Visitor Two (*avec much moaning*) Que serree—serra . . .
Victor (*dazedly*) H'mmmm?
Visitor Two (*translating, huskily*) "Whatever will be, will be!"

This is two much for Victor. With eyes still on Visitor Two, and phone in hand, he begins to sink to his knees. Visitor Two gently raises him to an upright position

(*Huskily, indicating the phone*) Tell them.
Victor H'mm? Oh, yes—yes, of course! (*Into the phone*) Are you still there? Oh, good! Well, I just wanted to say—to say—Que serree—serra. Good-bye! (*He replaces the receiver, unconsciously spins round twice, then clutches the table for support*)
Visitor Two (*composed, sexy*) Aren't you going to ask me to sit down?
Victor (*ecstatically*) Oh, I am! I am! (*He waves his hand towards a chair*) Do! Do!

But Visitor Two moves to the settee and sits at the far end of it

(*Almost dancing*) Er—er—can I get you something to drink?

Housekeeper Wanted

A Martini? A "Sidecar"? "Devil's Glory"?... A milk stout? A stout milk...?
Visitor Two (*huskily*) Not now. (*After a "come hither" look; softly*) Afterwards.

Victor again spins round twice, clutching his head, then a chair for support

Don't you think you ought to sit down—before you fall, I mean?
Victor (*dazedly*) Oh, I do! I do! (*He makes to sit on a chair, misses it and almost sits on the floor*)
Visitor Two (*seductively*) Wouldn't you be more—comfortable over here? (*She pats the settee*)
Victor Oh, I would! I would!
Visitor Two Then—why not?
Victor (*burbling*) Why not? Why not? (*He totters to the settee*)

Visitor Two takes one of his hands and gently draws him down to the settee. Victor nervously slides to the other end

Visitor Two (*noticing this*) I'm not going to bite you, you know.
Victor (*disappointed*) Oh, aren't you?

Visitor Two stretches out her hand, takes his and draws him nearer

Visitor Two (*purring*) There! That's better, isn't it?
Victor Oh, it is! It is!
Visitor Two Well, now...
Victor Oh, *very* well, now!
Visitor Two (*huskily*) We must get down to business, mustn't we?
Victor Oh, we must! We must! (*He puts his arm out to slip it around her*)
Visitor Two (*smiling but putting his arm down by his side*) I mean —*real* business.
Victor (*muttering*) That's what I *thought* you meant!
Visitor Two (*softly*) Right! Then you begin.

Victor again puts his arm out to put round her but pulls up
Victor You mean—to *talk*...?
Visitor Two (*beaming at him*) To talk.
Victor To talk. (*But his eyes are glued on her bosoms*) Er—yes— well—er—yes, well—er—yes, *well—well*...

Visitor Two Well, what?
Victor Well, I wish I had my dark glasses. (*He rubs his eyes*) So distracting.
Visitor Two (*laying a hand on his shoulder*) Shall—*I* begin . . . ?
Victor To talk?
Visitor Two To talk.
Victor Do! Do!
Visitor Two Well, then. The Bureau told me everything you'd require of me.
Victor (*eyes on bosom*) I *can't* believe *that!*
Visitor Two Of course, you'll want to see my references.
Victor I *can* see them——

Visitor Two raises her eyebrows

(*Gulping*) —*later!*
Visitor Two There are two . . .
Victor (*breaking in*) I know! I know!
Visitor Two Two things I ought to tell you.
Victor Tell! Tell!
Visitor Two I have a terrible confession to make—something you must know.
Victor What?
Visitor Two I'm ashamed to admit it, but—I'm—I'm . . .
Victor (*horrified*) You're *not?*
Visitor Two I'm no good at cooking.
Victor (*after a gasp of relief*) Cooking! Pah! What does that matter? I mean—I mean—with all your *other* qualifications! I would never *dream* of asking you to *cook!* In any case, you won't have the time! *I* will cook for both of us.
Visitor Two I have to be very careful what I eat—my figure, you see.
Victor I see—(*seeing*)—most clearly. Don't worry, I will cook you the most delectable dishes.
Visitor Two (*cooing*) You will?
Victor Full of Eastern Promise! Er—bacon and eggs—er—eggs and bacon—sausages—toast—cornflakes—black puddings . . .
Visitor Two Angel! (*She kisses the top of his head*)

Victor slides off the settee on to the floor in ecstacy. Visitor Two gently helps him back on to the settee but manœuvres him so that he

Housekeeper Wanted

is lying on the settee, legs over the end of it, and his head on her lap

(*Softly*) Better?

Victor's feet, over the end of the settee, wiggle their approval

Then we'll go a little further, shall we?

Victor (*eagerly*) Yes, let's!

Victor immediately tries to embrace her from his lying position

Visitor Two (*putting his arms down*) With our talk.
Victor (*almost sadly*) I'm looking—er—listening.
Visitor Two You live—alone?
Victor (*gulping*) 'Mmmmmmmpps!
Visitor Two And you're out—all day?
Victor I shan't be! Not for a single moment!
Visitor Two But—your work?
Victor I'm self-employed.
Visitor Two What at?
Victor I'm a writer.
Visitor Two A writer! How—romantic! (*Stroking his hair*) Tell me—*what* do you write?
Victor Furniture catalogues.

Visitor Two stops stroking his hair

Visitor Two (*somewhat ruffled*) But you won't be here—*all* the time?
Victor Why go hunting when you've food in the larder?
Visitor Two But—week-ends—will you be here then?
Victor I shall make a point of it.
Visitor Two (*disconcerted*) Oh!
Victor Why—what . . . ?
Visitor Two Er—are you broadminded?
Victor It's my intention to show you just *how* broadminded I am. Shall I do it *now*?
Visitor Two You see—I have a—a friend—who likes to come and see me most week-ends.
Victor Well, why not?
Visitor Two (*surprised*) You don't mind?
Victor Why should I? There's a spare bedroom!
Visitor Two How many bedrooms have you?

Victor Well—er—two. She can have the other one.
Visitor Two She?
Victor Your friend.
Visitor Two (*hesitantly*) She's—a "he".
Victor (*coming quickly to a sitting position*) What?
Visitor Two (*losing some of her "composure"*) Yes. You see—you see . . .
Victor (*somewhat stiffly*) You flatter me. At the moment, I *don't* see at all.
Visitor Two Well—poor Fred . . .
Victor Fred?
Visitor Two Poor Fred . . .
Victor (*irritably*) All right, *poor* Fred. What about him?
Visitor Two He's very unhappy.
Victor *Is* he?
Visitor Two Very. He lives in Pudsey.
Victor Pud . . . ? Where the hell's Pudsey?
Visitor Two Yorkshire. Somewhere north of Finsbury Park.
Victor Well, what about it?
Visitor Two Well, how would you like to live in Pudsey—with your *wife?*
Victor I'd hate it.
Visitor Two Well, so does Fred.
Victor Therefore . . . ?
Visitor Two Every now and again—once a month, in fact—he likes to get away from Pudsey.
Victor *And* his wife.
Visitor Two Naturally.
Victor And—naturally—he likes to spend the week-end with *you?*
Victor Two Naturally. I mean—it's natural, isn't it?
Victor It is far from natural. (*Recollecting*) But—once a month, you said?
Visitor Two Yes.
Victor But you also said "most week-ends".
Visitor Two Yes—but—you see—there's—another friend.
Victor (*bounding off the settee with a yelp*) Another?
Visitor Two (*nodding*) Poor Angus.
Victor Poor *Angus?*
Visitor Two (*nodding*) From Auchtermuchty.

Housekeeper Wanted

Victor (*wildly*) Auchter... Auchter... God! I've got lock-jaw!
Visitor Two It's in Scotland.
Victor And I presume poor Angus lives there—with *his* wife—and likes to get away from them both now and again.
Visitor Two (*nodding*) Once a month.
Victor (*bitterly*) *Naturally!*
Visitor Two (*with a big sigh*) He's very sweet, Angus.
Victor Plays the bagpipes, I suppose!
Visitor Two (*with an even bigger sigh*) He plays divinely!
Victor Hah!
Visitor Two (*with meaning*) But *not* the bagpipes.
Victor (*disgusted*) T'chah!
Victor Two And you should see his kilt!
Victor (*with feigned surprise*) Oh, you see him *dressed* occasionally?

Visitor Two gives him a big knowing smile

(*Pacing up and down, shocked*) Ooh! (*Stopping and ticking off his fingers*) Poor Fred once a month. Poor Angus once a month. (*Turning to Visitor Two*) That still leaves you with two weekends vacant.

Visitor Two Yes, but you see—there's poor Ev-*an*.
Victor (*babbling*) Ev... Ev-*an*?
Visitor Two From Pwllheli.
Victor From...
Visitor Two In Wales.
Victor (*pacing up and down, shocked*) Ooooohh! (*Stopping pacing and ticking off on his fingers*) Poor Fred once a month. Poor Angus once a month—and now...
Visitor Two Poor Ev-*an* is very sad—look you!
Victor (*sneering*) Location and wife trouble, I suppose?
Visitor Two Indeed to goodness, yes. His wife—she's terrible. Sings the same song all day long, Ev-*an* says.
Victor What...? (*He shakes his head despairingly as he stops and stares at Visitor Two*)
Visitor Two Well—as Ev-*an* says. (*With a very Welsh accent*) "What is the point of singing 'Home to our mountains we are *returning*' from morning till night, when she has never left the bloody things?

Victor resumes pacing and fuming

(*With a sigh*) Poor Ev-*an!*

Victor (*at last coming over to Visitor Two, raging*) There's still one week-end not accounted for? Don't—*don't* say you're going to tell me about—about—Shamus from—*Ballymurphy?*
Visitor Two (*smoothly*) I won't, if you don't want me to, but I was going to mention him.
Victor (*almost in a scream*) Aaaaaah! (*He starts more pacing*)
Visitor Two But he isn't from Ballymurphy.
Victor (*stopping*) Not . . . ?
Visitor Two (*smoothly*) No, *Ballygoyne.* (*After a slight pause*) Poor Shamus!

Victor marches up to the door, opens it, and turns to Visitor Two

Victor (*with a dramatic gesture*) Out!
Visitor Two (*startled*) What?
Victor (*dramatic gesture*) OUT!!
Visitor Two (*rising*) But—you haven't seen my references—not properly.
Victor (*striding down to her*) I've seen all I want to see of them— properly or *im*properly. (*With a dramatic gesture*) OUT!
Visitor Two (*beginning to plead*) You're being very—unreasonable.

They move to the door in stages during the following

Victor (*stuttering*) Un—un—UN . . . ! Fred—Angus—Ev*an—* Shamus—UNREASONABLE! (*With a dramatic gesture*) OUT!
Visitor Two But it would only be on *Fridays, Saturdays* and *Sundays* . . .
Victor ONLY!!! (*With a dramatic gesture*) OUT!!
Visitor Two And, of course, I should expect Mondays off.
Victor And, by God, you'd need 'em! (*With a dramatic gesture*) OUT!
Visitor Two (*seductively*) And think of *Tuesdays, Wednesdays* and *Thursdays!!!*
Victor OUT! OUT! *OUT!!!*
Visitor Two (*now in the doorway, turning to Victor*) The more I see of men, and heaven knows, there isn't much of them I *don't* see—the less I understand them!

Housekeeper Wanted

Visitor Two sweeps off through the door

Victor turns angrily away, paces the room for a moment, then goes to the drinks table and tries to coax a few drops out of an empty bottle, but in vain. He looks round the room in despair and then moves to the radio

Victor (*turning on the radio*) Something to cheer myself up!

The radio, immediately after he has spoken, gives out loudly the first few bars from the "Dead March in Saul". Victor does not immediately recognize the tune then, as he does so, he gives a cry of terror and dashes to the radio to turn it off

Aaaaaaaah! (*He swings away from the radio and begins to pace again, away from the door. At the end of his first cross of the stage, he turns to face the door*)

A tall, thin, ashen-faced woman, dressed in black from head to foot, is standing in the doorway—Visitor Three. The woman carries a black shopping bag in her black gloved hands. She stands quite still in the doorway—a blank expression on her face

Aaah! (*Still in a "state"*) What—who . . . ? (*Almost in a panic*) Madam, I assure you, I always—ALWAYS drive with *extreme* care.

Visitor Three (*it is a statement*) You were expecting me.
Victor Was I?
Visitor Three Yes.
Victor Oh?
Visitor Three Not just yet, perhaps—but—eventually.
Victor (*puzzled*) Ah, yes, the "Confidence" people have sent you along. They must've done. (*Muttering*) Who else *would?* (*Very conscious of Visitor Three's stillness*) Well—er—do come in. I mean—you mustn't stand out there in that draughty corridor; you'll catch your death . . . (*His voice tails away*)
Visitor Three (*smoothly*) No. I shan't catch *mine.*

Victor gives a little jump, puzzled by her remark

Victor Er—er . . . (*He motions her to come in*)

Visitor Three takes two deliberate steps into the room, then stops. Immediately there is heard the one, solitary, loud toll of a deep church bell. A large gong

>(*With a definite yelp*) Aaaaah! (*He spins round two or three times*)

Visitor Three stands silent and unmoved

>(*Recovering slightly*) Oh my . . . ! Oh my . . . ! (*Looking at Visitor Three apprehensively*) Do forgive me, but—for a moment I thought . . . ! Oh—my! Oh my! But of course, I see now! (*Pointing to the window*) The church clock—across the way—been out of order—hasn't struck a note for three years—but just now—as you came in . . . (*Wiping brow*) Oh—my! Oh—my! (*He looks at Visitor Three's face—it is a blank. Weakly*) Perhaps they're repairing it at last. (*He moves to the window and looks out*) Oh, yes, they *are!* There's a van outside the church—says "Johnson Brothers—Watch Repairers". (*He moves back into the room*) Oh my! Oh my! Silly me! Gave me quite a turn!

Visitor Three (*almost with satisfaction*) Your nerves—they're bad.
Victor (*blinking*) Are they?
Visitor Three! *Yes.*
Victor *Oh!*
Visitor Three And your heart—it isn't good.
Victor Isn't it?
Visitor Three No.
Victor *Oh!*
Visitor Three There's a blueness about the nostrils . . .
Victor (*nervously*) A . . .
Visitor Three A glassy glaze in the eyes—a waxen pallor on the . . . (*Breaking off*) But I mustn't go on. I might depress you.
Victor (*with airy sarcasm*) Oh, I don't *know* . . . (*Weakly, after tottering to the table and leaning on it with one hand*) I'm pretty tough, really!

Visitor Three gives a hollow mirthless laugh

>(*Hearing it*) Aaaah! (*He clutches the table with both hands; weakly*) Was that a rattlesnake, or . . . ?

Housekeeper Wanted

Visitor Three (*flatly*) It was me. I couldn't resist laughing.

Victor tries to speak but cannot get the words out

"I'm pretty tough"—that's what the Major said! In fact, the very last words he *did* say.
Victor The—er—the Major?
Visitor Three My late employer.
Victor The . . . Oh, you've *left* him?
Visitor Three No. He left me.
Victor Oh!
Visitor Three Yes—five hundred pounds. (*After a slight pause*) Most satisfactory.
Victor You mean he—er—er . . . (*He waves his hand vaguely*)
Visitor Three (*nodding*) Yes—he passed on.
Victor (*gulping*) Peacefully, I hope?
Visitor Three (*nodding*) I gave him all the help I could. Yes, I take great credit for the fact that he—er—went—happily.
Victor (*gulping again*) How—er—happily?
Visitor Three Eating one of my Cremation Crumpets.
Victor (*goggling*) Your . . . ?
Visitor Three That's what I call them. (*With a "smile"*) A little *joke*, you know.
Victor Do I?
Visitor Three The Major couldn't resist them. The times I said to him, "Major, they'll be the death of you," and . . .
Victor They *were*.
Visitor Three It shows one should *never* jest, doesn't it?
Victor Oh, it *does*.
Visitor Three Perhaps I shall make *you* some one day.
Victor (*anxiously*) You *are*—jesting, I hope?
Visitor Three Now—enough of this idle chatter! We have lots to discuss, haven't we? There is a little matter of—er . . .
Victor Of what?
Visitor Three References.
Victor (*surprised*) Oh, you *believe* in them?
Visitor Three I *insist* on them!
Victor Oh, that's fine! (*After a slight expectant pause*) So—if you will . . . (*He extends his hand slightly*)
Visitor Three (*blankly*) Will what?
Victor (*patiently*) The references—where are they?

Visitor Three How should I know? Where do you keep them?
Victor (*blankly*) Where do *I* . . . ? You mean—*you* want references—from *me*?
Visitor Three You don't object?
Victor But—references from whom? My solicitor?
Visitor Three No.
Victor Doctor?
Visitor Three No.
Victor Bank manager?
Visitor Three *Yes*.
Victor I—I—er—*most* embarrassing!
Visitor Three For you—or him?
Victor I—I—I'll see what I can do—that is—*if* . . .
Visitor Three Thank you. I like to know that my—gentlemen are *sound*.
Victor (*after thumping his chest heartily and stretching his arms vigorously*) But I am! Sound as a bell!
Visitor Three *Financially!*
Victor You insist on that?
Visitor Three One cannot afford to work for—no reward, can one?
Victor But so long as one knows that one's salary is—sure?
Visitor Three One has to think beyond *that*, hasn't one?
Victor Has one?
Visitor Three *This* one has.
Victor Oh!
Visitor Three I work on a "long term policy".
Victor Long . . . ?
Visitor Three But making it as short as possible.
Victor (*puzzled*) I don't quite . . .
Visitor Three For instance—the Vicar—I was only in his employment for three months.
Victor The—Vicar?
Visitor Three Well—the *Canon*—actually.
Victor Er—what happened to him?
Visitor Three He went off.
Victor (*gulping*) How?
Visitor Three Like the others—happily.
Victor (*horrified*) The *oth* . . . ?
Visitor Three (*breaking in, serenely*) The *dear* Canon! I shall always remember! It was Easter Sunday.

Victor Fancy!
Visitor Three After supper.
Victor Er—"Cremation Crumpets"?
Visitor Three (*after shaking her head*) He preferred my "Coffin Consommé".
Victor "Coffin . . . ?"
Visitor Three That's what I call it. Another of my little jokes
Victor (*heavily*) You *are* a one!
Visitor Three Er—where were we? I forget.
Victor The Coffin Consommé had just finished the Canon. (*Then quickly*) I mean—the Canon had just finished the Coffin Consommé.
Visitor Three Ah yea! And he was in his study—counting the Easter collections.
Victor How pleasant!
Visitor Three *Very* pleasant! They were particularly large that year.
Victor And—what happened?
Visitor Three I made so bold as to interrupt and ask him to come into the kitchen for a moment.
Victor And he came?
Visitor Three For the *briefest* of moments, yes.
Victor Why—what . . . ?
Visitor Three As he stepped into the kitchen he also stepped on a banana skin which—somehow—*happened* to be on the floor.
Victor And . . . ?
Visitor Three He fell. (*Her hand goes unobtrusively into her bag*)
Victor On the floor, naturally.
Visitor Three Not quite! On to a carving-knife which I *happened* to be holding in my hand.

Visitor Three produces a knife from her bag

Victor (*aghast*) Oh, my . . . !
Visitor Three I kept it as a souvenir.

Victor gives a yelp and staggers

Visitor Three (*smoothly*) Don't fall!
Victor (*leaping away*) Aaaah!
Visitor Three (*thumbing the blade of the knife*) Poor Canon! It was rather tragic.

Victor (*aghast*) Rather . . . ?
Visitor Three But—it had its bright side.
Victor Had it?
Visitor Three (*smoothly*) Yes. A quite satisfactory legacy—and the Easter collections totalled ninety-five pounds and two new pence.
Victor (*hardly realizing what he is saying*) Ninety-five pounds and . . .
Visitor Three We'd just gone over to decimal currency.
Victor (*almost gibbering*) I—I . . . (*He is about to sink into a chair*)
Visitor Three (*approaching him, carving-knife still in hand*) Well, now!

Victor leaps to his feet

> (*Nonchalantly placing the carving-knife point on one of Victor's waistcoat buttons*) To business!

Victor (*with a yelp*) Aaaaaaah!
Visitor Three Do you fancy my Cremation Crumpets?
Victor (*very much aware of the knife on his tummy*) Oh, I do!
Visitor Three And the Coffin Consommé?
Victor I'd adore it, but . . .
Visitor Three And, of course, there's my last resort—my Mortuary Meringues.
Victor Mortuary . . . ?
Visitor Three Yet another of my little jokes.

Victor goes into a longish spell of hollow phoney laughter

Victor (*at last; grimly*) Oh, do stop! I shall die laughing.
Visitor Three (*to herself*) H'mm! That's an idea! Less messy!
Victor But I must be truthful. You'd never accept the job.
Visitor Three Why not?
Victor My references—hopeless! My bank manager would tell you—I haven't a penny in the world!
Visitor Three (*sharply*) What!
Victor Worse. I'm minus several pennies. I'm overdrawn—in the red.
Visitor Three Are you telling me I've been wasting my time?
Victor I'm afraid so.

Housekeeper Wanted

Visitor Three T'chah! (*She quickly replaces the knife in her bag, takes out a small notebook and begins searching through it*)
Victor (*watching; interested*) What . . . ?
Visitor Three (*thinking aloud*) What's his address? If I hurry I might be in time.
Victor Who—er . . . ?
Visitor Three He's wanting a housekeeper, and—(*finding her place*)—oh, here we are!
Victor But—who . . . ?
Visitor Three (*studying the book*) The Dean of Saint Paul's.

(*Closing the book and preparing to depart*)

Victor The Dean of . . . ? But I doubt if he's got much collatoral!
Visitor Three (*sharply, as she moves to the door*) Don't talk nonsense! There's the Communion plate, isn't there? Solid gold, they tell me! *Good* morning!

Visitor Three departs quickly

Victor spins round twice, clutching his head

Victor (*muttering*) I can't take much more of this! I can't! I can't! (*He goes to the drinks table*) Drink! The only answer! (*He picks up the whisky bottle, then remembers it is empty*) Damn! (*He picks up the sherry bottle*) And blast! (*He puts down the sherry bottle*) There's *no* answer! (*He totters away from the table*) Victor, my lad, you're losing your grip. (*He holds out his shaking hands and looks at them*) You're losing your confidence. (*With a yelp*) Confidence! (*He rushes to the phone, picks up the receiver and begins to dial a number*)

As Victor begins to speak into the phone, a young woman, Victor's wife—Visitor Four!—comes into the doorway. She is attractive, smartly dressed, and wears a small but striking hat. She carries a largish shopping bag

On seeing Victor—with his back to her—she gives a disdainful toss of the head, then goes straight down to the front of the settee, kneels down by it and gropes under it with one hand and eventually produces—one at a time—a pair of lady's shoes which she puts into the shopping bag. She then moves to a table away from the telephone, bends over a drawer in it—her back to Victor—and searches through it, putting the odd item into her bag. Meanwhile Victor, having dialled, waits a moment or two, unaware of the fact that he is not alone. He speaks into the phone

(*Almost viciously*) Is that "Confidence *Undependable*, Unashamed, and totally *Unscrupulous* Ltd"? . . . It is! Well, I have something to say to you! I . . . What? Never mind who I am! That's no concern of yours—not any more it isn't! I requested you to send me a housekeeper—a white-haired angel who would attend to my every need. A white-haired angel I asked for, and what have you sent me so far? A *dipsomaniac* a *sex maniac*, and a *homicidal maniac!* All I'm waiting for now is a *kleptomaniac*. (*He turns and sees his wife bending over a drawer, but as only her posterior is presented to him, not her face, he does not recognize her. With a yelp*) And—my God—she's arrived! (*He slams down the receiver and leaps across the room to behind his wife, shouting*) Hey! What d'you think you're . . . ?

His wife, without straightening up, turns and looks at him disdainfully

(*With a yelp*) You!
Wife (*curtly*) Yes! (*She turns to the drawer*)
Victor (*gaping*) YOU!
Wife (*without turning*) Yes!
Victor (*stronger*) YOU!!!
Wife (*half turning; witheringly*) Shall I say "no", to break the monotony?
Victor (*dramatically*) This is the end!
Wife (*calmly*) It is not! It's only the beginning. I shall be half an hour yet. (*She bends over the drawer, more or less presenting her posterior to Victor*)
Victor (*unconsciously looking at her posterior*) How dare you show your—your face in this house again? (*He realizes where he has been looking, gives a grunt of exasperation and moves away slightly*)
Wife (*witheringly*) I'm come to collect the remainder of my belongings.
Victor (*almost growling*) Oh, *have* you?

Housekeeper Wanted

Wife I have. Any objections?
Victor None whatsoever. In fact, if you leave any, I shall charge you storage! (*With a grand gesture*) Go on! Go on! Get them! But I reserve the right to see that they *are* yours and not mine!

His Wife takes something out of the drawer

(*Suddenly*) What's that? What have you got there?
Wife (*opening her hand*) A lipstick. (*Witheringly*) Yours?
Victor (*fuming*) T'chah! (*Waving his hand*) Get on! Get on! Don't waste my time.
Wife And talking of time—it's eleven o'clock, so you can invite me to have a sherry if you don't mind.
Victor (*automatically moving to the drinks table*) Sherry ... (*Pulling up, indignantly*) I *do* mind, and I will not invite you to have a sherry. Just get on with—ransacking my drawers.
Wife (*returning to the drawers*) That reminds me—did you remember to change yours?
Victor My what?
Wife Your drawers.
Victor *What?*
Wife Your underpants. I told you yesterday, before I left the house, they had a hole in the seat. Did you change them?
Victor I refuse to discuss my underwear with a complete and utter stranger.

His Wife takes a small photograph out of the drawer

(*Almost pouncing*) What's that? I'm sure it's mine.
Wife (*coolly*) It's a photograph of mother.
Victor Then it's yours. (*He moves away, ruffled*) And by the way —how is the old—(*he pulls up*)—how *is* your mother?
Wife Very relieved.
Victor Relieved?
Wife That I have, *at last*, see the light!
Victor You mean you've—joined the Salvation Army?
Wife I have seen you for what you really are.
Victor That being?
Wife Everything you can think of that a lady wouldn't mention.

(*She picks up a silver cigarette box from the top of the drawers*)

Victor (*seeing this; grandly*) Just a minute! (*With great satisfaction*) Aaaaah! Now that *is* mine!
Wife (*coldly*) *I* bought it for you last Christmas, didn't I?
Victor Yes.
Wife (*practically*) Yes. So it's mine. (*The box disappears into the bag*)
Victor (*fuming*) Oooooooh! (*He moves, away, then turns. Suddenly, pointing*) That stupid hat you're wearing—I paid for that, didn't I?
Wife What? Of course you did.
Victor Thanks very much. (*He snatches the hat from her head and automatically puts it on his own*)
Wife (*icily*) As you wish, but—it doesn't suit you. (*She goes to the table and unconsciously puts her hands on it as she looks at it*)
Victor (*still wearing the hat, rushing across to her side*) That table's not going into your bag. That doesn't belong to you.
Wife Nor to you. It's very much the property of the "No Deposit Furnishing Company". (*She is looking around the room and suddenly sees "the" ornament*) Aaah (*Going towards it*) I'm sure you'll be *very glad* to say good-bye to *this*. (*She picks up the ornament*)
Victor (*with great "indignation"*) How—*dare*—you!
Wife (*ornament in hand, gaping at him*) What?
Victor (with greater "indignation") PUT—THAT—DOWN!
Wife (*babbling*) But—but . . .
Victor THIEF!
Wife *What?*
Victor THIEF! I've a good mind to dial nine-nine-nine!
Wife (*gaping at him*) Have you gone completely crazy, or are you losing your eyesight?
Victor To the best of my knowledge, neither.
Wife (*holding the ornament out; bewildered*) But—but *this* was Mother's birthday present to *you.*
Victor Nor have I lost my memory!
Wife But—yesterday you said you couldn't stand the sight of it!
Victor (*loftily*) What I *said* yesterday does not necessarily have to bear any relevance to what I *think* today.
Wife (*bewildered*) Obviously not! So what you are saying now *is* that you do like this—(*looking at ornament somewhat askance*) —*this*—er—*this*—er . . .

Housekeeper Wanted

Victor (*loftily again*) Am I? Thank you for saving me the trouble of speaking for myself. But you could be right. Perhaps I *do* like—(*pointing at the ornament*)—that—er—that—er . . .
Wife (*sharply*) Do you, or don't you? Answer me!
Victor Madam! I am not in the witness-box!
Wife You *don't* like it, do you?
Victor And I will not have you telling me what I like and dislike. (*He strides around*) As a matter of fact I—I—(*he gulps*)—I *do* like it.
Wife (*gaping*) You—you do? (*She looks at the ornament in horror*)
Victor (*gulping again*) Scouts' Honour! (*Seeing she is not looking at him, he quickly puts his hands together, looks heavenwards, obviously praying for forgiveness. He then gives a smart Scouts' —two-fingered—salute*)
Wife (*completely flummoxed*) But—but you can't possibly live with *this!*
Victor And why not?
Wife (*holding out the ornament*) Well—*look* at it!
Victor (*with "emotion"*) I have looked at it—all through the night.
Wife No wonder you look boss-eyed! I—I can't believe—you're just *saying* . . . You don't like it, do you?
Victor (*going to town*) "Like?" Oh, woman! Woman! One doesn't just "like" a work of art. One worships. (*He goes quickly down on his knees and prostrates himself Moslem fashion before the ornament*)
Wife But—this isn't a work of art. It *can't* be.
Victor Why not?
Wife Well—Mother bought it.
Victor (*still on his knees, again prostrating himself as he speaks*) The blessings of Allah be with her. May her hot-water bottle never leak!
Wife (*almost emotionally*) But—don't you realize . . . ? We need never have quarrelled at all. (*Irritably*) Oh, for goodness' sake, don't grovel about down there. (*She gives him a sharpish prod with her foot*)
Victor (*with a little yelp*) Ouch! (*He gets to his feet quickly*)
Wife (*repeating, with much sentiment*) We need never have quarrelled at all.

Victor Que serree serra.
Wife What?
Victor (*at once, acutely embarrassed*) Er—forget it!
Wife (*almost tearfully*) If you hadn't pretended you didn't like it!

Victor gives a big shrug of the shoulders

(*Tearfully*) And if I hadn't pretended I *did* . . . !
Victor waves a hand airily in the air and walks to behind the settee (*In a burst*) Darling . . . I forgive you! (*She rushes to him behind the settee—ornament still in one hand*)

Victor *What?*
Wife (*wildly*) DARLING!!! (*She makes to embrace him and accidentally drops the ornament behind the settee. Alarmed*) Oh!

Victor moves one step—there is a crunching sound

(*Looking down in horror*) I've—dropped it! (*She immediately disappears behind the settee*)
Victor (*looking straight out towards the audience—a big beaming smile on his face. Slowly*) And *I've*—TRODDEN on it!

His Wife appears behind the settee with the broken pieces of ornament in her hands. These, of course, have been planted behind the settee to save breaking a new ornament during a production

Wife (*shaken*) Darling—it doesn't matter.
Victor (*indignantly*) Not matter? *Not* matter?
Wife I know just where Mother bought it and they have hundreds more. (*Brightening*) I'll go and get one right away——
Victor (*with a yelp*) What?
Wife (*unheeding*) —and then, darling—and then—we'll live happily together ever after. (*She gives him a big kiss and puts the broken pieces of ornament into his hands*) DARLING!

His Wife dashes out through the door

Victor, with the bits of ornament in his hands, is almost at bursting point. He spins round twice, automatically puts his hands to his head, the broken pieces drop to the floor

Victor (*wildly*) Aaaah!

His Wife rushes in through the door

Wife (*excitedly*) Darling!

Victor almost leaps in the air, then spins round twice

Victor Aaaaaah!
Wife (*coming quickly to his side and holding out a hand*) Two pounds, fifty.
Victor What?
Wife To buy the new ornament—two pounds, fifty.
Victor (*babbling*) I—I—I—I . . . (*Gulping*) My wallet—I don't know where it is.
Wife (*easily*) I do. (*She quickly extracts a wallet from Victor's hip pocket*)
Victor (*as she does this*) Aaaaah!
Wife (*after taking a note from the wallet and looking at it quickly*) Oh! It's a five-pound note! (*Happily*) Never mind! I'll use it up somehow.

Victor whimpers

(*With enthusiasm*) Darling! (*She kisses him perfunctorily*)

After putting the wallet into his hand, the Wife dashes off through the door

Victor, still wearing the hat, spins round twice, then totters up to the telephone, sinks to his knees beside it, reaches dazedly for the receiver, then dials

Victor (*into the phone; croaking*) Is that the Confidence Unlimited Employment Bureau? . . . Well, listen. If you were thinking of sending along a *money*-maniac, don't bother. I've got one. She's come back to me—for life!

As Victor puts down the receiver—

the CURTAIN *falls*

FURNITURE AND PROPERTY LIST

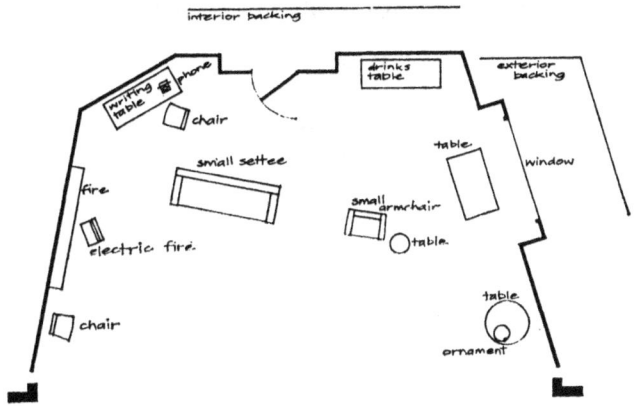

On stage: Settee. *Under it:* dustpan and brush
Small armchair
2 upright chairs
Occasional table beside armchair. *On it:* full ashtray
Drinks table. *On it:* bottle of whisky, bottle of sherry, soda syphon, glasses
Writing table. *On it:* telephone
Table in window. *On it:* radio, vase of flowers, silver cigarette box, small oddments ad lib. *In drawers:* small oddments ad lib., including photograph and lipstick
Occasional table (down L) *On it:* ugly ornament
Electric fire (not practical)
On floor behind settee: pieces of broken ornament
Carpet
Window curtains

Off stage: Shopping basket with whisky bottle **(Visitor One)**
Black shopping bag with carving-knife and small black notebook **(Visitor Three)**
Large shopping bag **(Visitor Four)**

Personal: **Victor:** handkerchief, wallet with £5 note
Visitor One: copy of *War Cry*, handkerchief

LIGHTING PLOT

Property fittings required: nil
Interior. A lounge

To open: General effect of a bright summer day
No cues

EFFECTS PLOT

Cue 1	**Victor:** "Just you wait." *Telephone rings*	(Page 2)
Cue 2	**Victor** turns on radio *Music—"Dead March in Saul", loud*	(Page 19)
Cue 3	**Victor** turns off radio *Music off*	(Page 19)
Cue 4	**Visitor Three** takes two steps into room and stops *Church bell tolls once, loudly*	(Page 19)

www.ingramcontent.com/pod-product-compliance
Lightning Source LLC
Chambersburg PA
CBHW070454050426
42450CB00012B/3268